LIBERTY & JUSTICE FOR ALL?

WILL HANSON

Liberty & Justice for All?

Copyright © 2020 Will Hanson

Produced and printed
by Stillwater River Publications.
All rights reserved. Written and produced in the
United States of America. This book may not be reproduced
or sold in any form without the expressed, written
permission of the author and publisher.

Visit our website at
www.StillwaterPress.com
for more information.

First Stillwater River Publications Edition

ISBN: 978-1-952521-43-0

Library of Congress Control Number: 2020916035

1 2 3 4 5 6 7 8 9 10

Written by Will Hanson
Published by Stillwater River Publications,
Pawtucket, RI, USA.

Publisher's Cataloging-In-Publication Data
(Prepared by The Donohue Group, Inc.)

Names: Hanson, Will, 1946- author.
Title: Liberty & justice for all? / Will Hanson.
Other Titles: Liberty and justice for all?
Description: First Stillwater River Publications edition. |
Pawtucket, RI, USA : Stillwater River Publications, [2020]
Identifiers: ISBN 9781952521430
Subjects: LCSH: Right and left (Political science)--
United States--History--21st century. | Polarization (Social
sciences)--United States--History--21st century. | United States--
Politics and government--21st century. | United States--
Social conditions--21st century.
Classification: LCC JK1717 .H36 2020 |
DDC 320.9730905--dc23

TEXT SET IN CRIMSON.

The views and opinions expressed
in this book are solely those of the author
and do not necessarily reflect the views
and opinions of the publisher.

To all victims of injustice, past, present, and future.

INTRODUCTION

This book was written as a result of the division and chaos that currently exists in the United States, and that has grown wider over the last four plus years. It is a division and chaos that was very predictable. I also wrote this book because of the affect these divisions have had on me personally, and I discovered some heightened awareness as to where we came from, where we are now, and where we might be going.

I love my country and I'm proud to be an American, but unfortunately I am not as proud as I used to be and I wanted to try to understand why. My usual "glass-three-quarters-full" attitude has become a "glass-three-quarters-empty" one—and not so much outwardly, but certainly internally.

Crimes, injustices, and bad behavior seemed to be magnified and come to the forefront and have overshadowed the good things. I am frustrated because of the actions of some people who, in my opinion, have been, are being, and will continue to be out of touch with common sense and common human decency.

Some of the things happening now are so disturbing that to try to help me understand, I decided to go back to look at the birth of our country and follow some of the events through our history—more specifically, the actions of white Americans during these events. I looked at some historical facts and other key elements of our society that I think most of us are all too complacent about. And I'm guilty of it, too.

So what happened? And why, after all these years, has it managed to somewhat alter my disposition and opinions about social issues and people in general? As you may have guessed, it was a political event, specifically the 2016 Presidential election. As it turned out though, that event was only the catalyst and tip of the iceberg. I got more focused and really had issues with the priorities and values of our government, our democracy, our justice system, and ourselves.

Admittedly, the problems in this country started way before the 2016 election and will remain with us during the 2020 election and well beyond. Regardless of who is in the White House, the real question is how focused are we as citizens and how focused are our elected officials who are there to help solve these problems?

I want to make it very clear that this is not a book about Republican vs. Democrat, Right vs. Left, Red vs. Blue, or Conservative vs. Liberal. It's about our country and our people, and it's about right and wrong, good and bad, and love and hate.

If you're not like me and already angry, you probably will be by the time you finish the book. (Either angry along with me, or angry at me.) Either way, I'm good with it because misery loves company. The book may not change any opinions, and I'm not sure yet whether writing it will help me understand more or just make me more frustrated. I'll let you know when it's done. I would also like to get back to enjoying my retirement years like I did before the "Fall of 2016."

1

MY EARLY YEARS

This book is certainly not about me, but I think it's important to give you some background. My life, from the beginning, can be described as very good, probably better than average with great loving and caring parents. We were middle class but certainly not upper middle class. My dad worked days and my mom worked the third shift for many years, and both worked until they were old enough to retire. The family was very close with great loving and caring aunts and uncles, too. I probably received more love and care than the average child, adolescent, and young adult. I was aware of it but didn't really appreciate it to the extent I should have because I was somewhat shielded from those less fortunate.

As a child, television was a novelty and many of the early shows and movies were about cowboys and Indians. The cowboys were the good guys, and the

Indians were the bad guys, of course. Like most other kids my age, I had my two six-shooters (toy guns) holstered and strapped to my waist for hours almost every day. It wasn't until Tonto and the Lone Ranger came along that I began to realize that all Indians may not be bad.

The good life continued for me as an adult, and I was able to recognize and appreciate it by the time I reached my mid-twenties. No one's life is perfect though. The ups greatly outweighed the downs and the downs were a direct result of the bad decisions I made and that I take full responsibility for.

We can never go backward however, so we move forward and hope to at least learn from the mistakes. As humans, we will all make them, but not learning from them is eliminating the only positive result. Unfortunately, humans in this country have been making the same mistakes for hundreds and hundreds of years and still haven't learned a fraction of what they should have from them.

Most of what I remember and can write about my early years started in the 1950s when I was in grammar school. I was actually in parochial schools for 14 years; nursery school, kindergarten, and grades 1 through 12. I can remember being in grammar school when I was asked "Who are the three people you would like to meet most in the world?" My answer was Ted Williams, the pope and the president. Ted has since died, and I would eventually lose my desire to meet the other two.

History was taught in school with more depth as we progressed through the grades, but even though I was getting a religious education, I never remember actually being taught the tragic details of what really happened to the American Indians or to Black people in this country. There were some facts in textbooks and some things we had to learn to pass a test, but truly no in-depth discussion to try to help us understand what they really went through. Some of those missing details would certainly come to light in the research I had to do for the next two chapters.

I imagine schools now provide more historical details than they did for me. I have the sense that back then, some white Americans didn't want to know all the details and others still thought what happened was OK. Some still do.

At home there was no open verbal aggression or hateful comments towards Indians, Blacks, or anyone else. I was never really exposed to any Black people until my late teens or early twenties. Social media consisted of radio, newspapers, and television with a limited number of channels. Reports of prejudice and bigotry, and the lynching and shooting of people because of their skin color, was difficult to understand or even comprehend. This was in the 50s and 60s yet in 2020 were still dealing with it?

So how have we, white Americans, dealt with people and issues from the beginning? Let's start with the period of time following the Revolutionary War and discuss the treatment of American Indians and African Americans starting with the birth of our country.

NATIVE AMERICANS

The Revolutionary War started in 1775 and the Declaration of Independence was signed in 1776. The war officially ended in 1781 and the final peace treaty was signed in 1783. Native Americans were obviously here before white settlers and it was or should have been their land, too. From the beginning, some white settlers tried to treat them fairly and some didn't. Some recognized that they were human beings and others didn't really care. Unfortunately, those who didn't care won.

By the early 1800s, a group of southern states was spearheading an attempt to move the Indians off of their land. Andrew Jackson, who was the president at the time and from the South, authorized The Indian Removal Act in 1830 to forcibly remove the Native Americans to land west of the Mississippi River. Somewhat surprisingly, the Cherokee Indians brought the issue to the Supreme Court and won. The court ruled in their favor and said the law was unconstitutional.

Despite this, settlers still took the Indians land and possessions and slaughtered many of them. Tribes that fought to protect their families and their land were dealt with severely, and Jackson failed to enforce the Supreme Court ruling. Eventually this resulted in their forced migration which is referred to as "The Trail of Tears" because of the hardships the Indians endured and the number who died when they were forced off their land, on foot, to the territory west.

> *After writing, reading, and thinking about the last paragraph, I realized that I had stopped and stared out the window for about five minutes before I continued. I certainly can't get into the heads of people who lived two hundred years ago or understand the culture or mentality. I can't even understand the culture or mentality of some people living today. As I continued on through these chapters, there would be many more pauses.*

Jackson's legacy may not be defined by this one act, but how many of us even knew about it? I didn't and look at the devastating effect it had on so many people. It's disappointing to think that 190 years ago we had a person who held the highest office in the country who thought he was above the law. Should we not expect anyone in that position to be held to the highest possible standards of honesty and integrity and to abide by the laws of the land? I don't know if Jackson was the first American president to think he was above the law, but I think we all know he wasn't the last. Is it possible that 190 years ago there was a travesty of justice done in this country that we didn't learn from? Yes, and countless others since.

As the years went by, there were many treaties made with the Indians that kept forcing them off their lands and farther west. As white settlers also pushed farther west there was eventually no land left. The Indian Appropriations Act in 1851 established the reservation system to help keep them under control. They were not even allowed to leave the reservations without permission. Conditions on the reservations were poor and their culture and religious beliefs were threatened by the expectations of white settlers and the government.

The Dawes Act of 1887 divided up reservation land making it even smaller, continuing to make life more miserable for the Indians.

Finally in 1934, the Indian Reorganization Act was formed to help Indians restore their culture. More land and financial aid were given to them and a system of tribal self-governing was implemented. The damage had been done, though, and done since the birth of our country. They would continue to suffer from poverty and poor living conditions and underfunded health care.

Throughout this whole sad saga, white settlers and political leaders saw the American Indians as inferior and felt they were a hindrance to economic progress. I guess we wanted to establish early on that it was all about the money. The end justified the means.

And just to be clear, going back to 1776, one of the main reasons white settlers wanted the land was to grow cotton.

AFRICAN AMERICANS

In the 17th and 18th Centuries, Black people were kidnapped from Africa and brought to the American colonies to work on tobacco farms and in cotton fields. They were forcibly removed from their country to be owned by white people and work as slaves in what is now our country.

Following the revolution and the birth of our nation in 1776, our forefathers, in their finite wisdom, addressed the importance of liberty and equality in the U.S. Constitution and Declaration of Independence. They also made slavery legal in all 13 colonies. You could own them, buy them, and sell them.

The Fugitive Slave Act of 1793 made it illegal for slaves to run away from their owners. In 1850, it was revised to include anyone helping slaves run away. The Underground Railroad was able to help about 100,000 escape to the north, but that was a very small fraction of those being held.

Prior to the Civil War, there were 19 free states where slavery was illegal and 15 slave states where slavery was legal. There were almost four million African American slaves at the time and the debate over slavery was the biggest reason for the Civil War. Lincoln was elected president in 1860 and eleven southern states seceded from the union. The Civil War started in 1861 to reunify the country and Lincoln issued the Emancipation Proclamation January 1, 1863 to make it clear that this unification would include freeing the slaves.

At the completion of the war in 1865, the 13th Amendment was passed abolishing slavery. That was followed by the 14th and 15th Amendments that granted citizenship and prohibited denying citizens the right to vote. These were all aimed at providing equality for African Americans, but obviously they were not effective enough to see that they were actually treated equally.

Following President Lincoln's assassination in 1865, Vice President Andrew Johnson, who was from Tennessee, had all the states ratify the 13th Amendment. But he allowed the states free rule and southern states developed Black Codes (also known as Jim Crow laws) that legalized racial segregation. These not only contributed to the birth of the KKK but restricted and denied rights to African Americans until the passage of the Civil Rights Act in 1964 **one hundred years later!**

So finally, we have a Civil Rights Act and we can all live happily ever after. If I was writing a fairy tale, I guess I could end this chapter right here. Unfortunately I can't.

Although the Civil Rights Act should have been the means to finally take legal actions against all forms of segregation and inequality, it would in no way change some people's opinions. Also, it should be noted that it passed the House and Senate by a vote total of 363 to 157. Even in 1964, over 40% of our congressman voted against it and civil unrest would continue for decades to come.

There was the Bloody Sunday march in Selma, Alabama in 1965. Martin Luther King was assassinated in Memphis in 1968. Countless Blacks along with white Americans who helped or sympathized with Blacks, were killed. As time went on there was some improvement, but how long should any person or group of people be expected to wait to be treated equally?

We can go back to Rodney King and fast forward to George Floyd and all the Black citizens in between who were injured or died because of the color of their skin. Is it really that difficult for any of us to understand the resentment of people who had to endure all of this? Apparently it is.

And there is an undeniable commonality with the struggles of Indians and Blacks in this country: the prejudice, greed, and entitlement of some white Americans.

4

THE INDUSTRIAL
REVOLUTION

In the years following the Civil War, advancements
in technology were moving quickly with steel, elec-
tricity, and automobiles. The rail systems were being
expanded, factories were being built, and there was
now a great dependency on coal.

America was booming and I guess it's only natural that a small number of Americans were acquiring
extraordinary wealth at the expense of the working
class. Chinese immigrants played a huge role in the
expansion of the railroads. It was dangerous work,
they were paid less than others doing the same jobs,
and hundreds died.

Conditions in the coal mines were extremely dangerous and unhealthy and miners were overworked
due to the high demand. The imbalance would
worsen, but there was some hope and someone who

would help deal with the injustices and the imbalance.

Before becoming vice president, Teddy Roosevelt had been police commissioner of New York City and then governor of New York. He was appointed police commissioner to help clean up crime and corruption and carried that effort over as governor. He had a reputation of being incorruptible, and although he was a Republican, he favored regulating big business. He had no problem taking on greedy and corrupt industrialists, bankers, and politicians.

He served under William McKinley as vice president in March of 1901 and then became President when McKinley was assassinated in September of the same year. This would become a nightmare for some of the country's big industrialists and they were well aware of it. Roosevelt had become popular with the people and some Republicans thought that having him as vice president might neutralize him somewhat. Much to their dismay, he was now president.

Roosevelt understood the importance and benefits of big business but felt that no businessman should be powerful enough to cripple the economy. He intervened in the coal miners' strike of 1902 when the miners and management couldn't come to an agreement. As the strike was threatening to shut down the coal supply for the winter, he met with both sides and eventually the miners got more money and shorter working hours.

He also went after J.P. Morgan, the country's most powerful financier, to put an end to monopolies and help control unfair pricing of goods and services. Roosevelt was a conservationist and responsible for many of the country's national parks and monuments as well as the preservation of forests and woodlands. He felt strongly about fairness for the average citizen and believed that the people should be in control of their own affairs.

What I admire most about him was his ability to make decisions based on what he thought was right for the majority of the American citizens. He wasn't influenced by party or by big business—an admirable trait. It is a trait that should be a priority with all our elected officials. A trait that seems to have been sidelined.

THE AMERICAN
"JUSTICE" SYSTEM

We obviously had a problem with our justice system starting in 1776 as we have seen in chapters two and three. Has it improved since then? Have we used the last 244 years to learn anything and to make it better, or have we been more innovative in finding ways to make it worse? That's unthinkable right? It should be, so let's examine it with just a few of the many examples.

Before we move on I want to be clear that I have a high degree of respect for the vast majority of police and law enforcement officials who put their lives on the line for us daily to combat crime and keep us safe. There is no question that we need them, defunding is not a solution, and their existence is critical. We all need to work together. It's a very difficult job that requires some leverage and understanding, but there should also be no question that negligence, overly aggressive tactics, or criminal acts should not be tolerated.

I believe strongly that the punishment should fit the crime and be severe enough to act as a deterrent for the future. I don't mean inhumane behavior, but prisoners are not generally going to be totally rehabilitated in prison so somehow we should take measures to ensure that if they get out, they won't want to go back (I'm referring to the guilty ones).

Some definitions of "Justice" from various sources include righteousness, fairness, equity, honor or treatment to support fair standards. These are all definitions that make sense, and as long as people are committing crimes or doing things that do not support fair standards, which will be forever, we need to have a good justice system.

How many times have judges given bail or light sentences for serious crimes? How many times have parole boards let dangerous criminals back out onto the streets to victimize someone else?

I have never been accused or convicted of a crime that I didn't commit. I have never been the victim of a crime who didn't receive the appropriate justice. I can, however, feel and have empathy for anyone who has and I can only imagine their anger and frustration.

Frequently, there are reports of people who have

been imprisoned for years or decades who are innocent. Some are victims of unfortunate circumstances where an eyewitness or jury got it wrong. That's not justice, but hopefully just honest mistakes that are sometimes difficult to avoid. Others, however, were put there by prejudiced law enforcement officials or prosecutors looking to close a case or further their careers. Some law enforcement officials were even paid or influenced to lie and withhold evidence.

Those are crimes, too, but when the truth is uncovered, where is the punishment and accountability? Maybe they should spend as much time in prison as the innocent victim did. But what they get is a slap on the wrist in comparison or sometimes no punishment at all. Maybe this would happen less frequently if the punishment fit the crime and they received a matching sentence.

For those of you who think I watch too much television, you're right, especially over the last few months. I'm not referring to fictional TV shows though. As of February 2020, there were 2,551 exonerations on the U.S. Wrongful Convictions List. The exonerated individuals had spent a total of 22,540 years in prison. And this does not include any innocent people still in prison or others we will never know about.

In addition to wrongful convictions, there are also people who should have been convicted, or reprimanded, or lost their jobs but didn't. I'm relatively certain just reading the previous sentence brought one or more names to the minds of everyone. There's no list for that, though, but the victims and their families are certainly well aware of who they are.

So many of these cases are a result of unscrupulous lawyers with little or no regard for the law or for justice. Lawyers who will either lie or bend the truth about their clients and the victims of their clients. And why? For the money. That's our justice system, and that's the morality of some attorneys and prosecutors.

THE CRASH OF 2008

The stock market and housing market crash of 2008 was devastating to many Americans, the stock market itself, and economies of other countries.

Here were the causes:
- Government's continued deregulation of financial institutions and regulators not doing their jobs.
- Policies of financial institutions.
- Predatory lending practices.

- Big bonuses to mortgage brokers who made risky loans.
- Inaccurate credit ratings on risky loans.

So what happened to those responsible? I'll quote Warren Buffet on the individuals leading those financial institutions: "They were doing some things that should have sent them to jail." And "they went away rich." But remember, George Floyd had to die because he was accused of trying to pass a counterfeit twenty-dollar bill?

Note: If you're interested in seeing who introduced the deregulation bill, and getting some background on him, you can look up the "Financial Services Modernization Act" of 1999.

SEX ABUSE

Catholic priests sexually abused children for decades. Bishops, cardinals, and popes were well aware of it, and what did they do about it? Not much. They moved the priests to other parishes. There have been thousands of accusations but only a small number actually prosecuted. Most of the offenders were either asked to resign or retire. Should this be viewed as a worldwide religious institution that should be charged with conspiracy?

JEFFREY DAHMER

We'll deal more with justice and injustice in some of the following chapters, but I'll end this chapter with an extremely disturbing example that goes back to 1991 and the Jeffery Dahmer case.

Dahmer's thirteenth victim was a 14-year-old boy. A woman saw the boy **outside, naked, beaten, and bleeding from the rectum.** He got away from Dahmer and she approached the boy to help him and called 911. Dahmer came out of his house and was trying to forcibly take the boy back with him, but the woman resisted and told him she had already called 911 for help. She was seventeen years old at the time but to her it was obvious that something was very wrong.

Two police officers arrived and Dahmer, who was also a convicted sex offender at the time, told them the boy was his gay lover and not underage. The officers said they believed him, and with no further investigation, decided to let Dahmer take the boy as the officers left. Dahmer later killed the boy and four more after him before he was finally caught. Dahmer said later that one of his victims was dead in his apartment at the time the officers questioned him.

Pause for a moment and consider what you think happened to those officers who should hold some degree of responsibility for the deaths of five people.

The truth is they were fired, appealed, and then reinstated with back pay. One eventually became president of the police union. There was one report that the other officer had actually been an interim police chief. Justice?

DEMOCRACY

Some definitions of democracy include:
1) A system of government by the whole population typically through elected representatives.
2) The practice and principles of social equity.
3) Control of an organization or group by the majority of its members.

So do we really have a democracy in this country or not? Let's look more into the definitions.
1) We do have a system of government that operates through elected representatives. It is implied, however, that those representatives are representing our interests. Are they really? Or are they representing their own interests and/ or the interests of other individuals or groups?
2) We have the principles of social equity but obviously not the practice. I don't think there

is much to debate on this, but only recognize the sad truth that some people don't care about it. Though not the majority (I hope).

3) The "organization" is certainly not always controlled by the majority.

EXAMPLES

One of the most obvious examples is the presidential election which is decided by the Electoral College and not the popular vote. I don't care if it's a Republican or a Democrat or a candidate we voted for or not. If the candidate with the least votes gets to lead this country for four years, the country is not controlled by the majority.

Also, all 50 states do not choose the number of Electoral College votes the same way. Is this one country or not? For something as important as a presidential election, shouldn't we all be playing by the same rules?

2016 Presidential Election Results
Democratic Candidate: 65,853,514
Republican Candidate: 62,984,828

GUN CONTROL

Although I'm not in favor of taking away the guns of responsible law-abiding citizens, I do feel strongly that current gun laws need to be addressed. I also think that not everyone is as attentive to other parts of the Constitution as they are to the 2nd Amendment. I don't think it was meant to be like a menu where you pick what you want and forget about the rest.

The vast majority of U.S. citizens are in favor of some form of gun control. Every day people are killed in this country but individual killings are unfortunately all too commonplace to receive any national attention. Only when we have mass shootings is there some form of attention, acknowledgement, the same boiler plate message of sympathy "our thoughts and prayers are with the victims and their families," and a conversation about addressing the problem, and even then nothing is done.

So many of us thought that Sandy Hook would be the turning point, and there is a great deal of frustration as very little changes and the same problems continue to exist. Why? Because the NRA steps in and our representatives decide to represent them and not us.

THE 2017 TAX CUT BILL

Everyone is aware of the wealth imbalance in this country. The 2017 tax cut bill gave a three percent tax reduction to the average American (the majority) and a fourteen percent tax reduction to corporations.

Of course, everyone likes tax cuts and I'm not complaining about the three percent reduction in itself. I think the corporate tax should have been reduced, too, but what's the bottom line of the entire bill?

Most Americans benefited from the three percent tax reduction, but the fourteen percent reduction that went to corporations would also save the President, his family, and many of his friends and campaign contributors multiple millions of dollars every year. And your three percent is only good for 10 years. Not their fourteen percent, though.

With the tax reductions and other deductions in the bill, The Tax Policy Center estimates that by 2027, almost eighty-three percent of the total tax reductions will go to the top one percent richest people in the country. If those figures are accurate, most of us should have a real concern. I'm somewhere in the forgotten ninety-nine percent. How about you? And they want us to believe that this is supposed to somehow magically trickle down to the rest of us. You can be sure that most of it will trickle right into their pockets.

MEDICARE MODERNIZATION ACT

There is actually a law that prohibits the Secretary of the Department of Health and Human Services from negotiating prices with drug companies for Medicare. The law was passed in 2003 with what they actually call "a noninterference clause." It is estimated that changing this law could save well over 10 billion dollars annually and this has been going on now for seventeen years. Why?

The vast majority of Americans who know about it want it changed (of course) with the probable exception of the drug companies and their lobbyists. I'm comfortable with predicting that Americans who don't know about it would like to see it changed, too. You don't think the drug companies had anything to do with the 2003 law, do you? I wonder how many other laws there are like this that we're not aware of.

Lobbying: An attempt by private interest groups to influence government decisions and votes of legislatures. And this is legal? Is bribery legal?

Healthcare in the U.S. needs to be addressed for everyone's sake. We know drug costs are too high and we know why. So fix it, Congress. Most companies offer healthcare plans and, as I do understand the need to balance the books and make profits, there is also a need to do it responsibly. As healthcare costs go up, companies require more out of pocket costs from their employees and hire more temporary or part-time employees to avoid paying for their health-care. Many of the temporary agencies don't provide health to them either. Those employees are helping to bring profits to those companies and agencies but where do they get healthcare from and how much is it going to cost them?

Our government needs to find a sensible solution that makes this work more fairly for employees and employers. Maybe Congress could start by offering us the option of their healthcare plan and their co-pay. I don't know what it is but it would be like leading by example.

7

MONEY, POWER, ENTITLEMENT, CORRUPTION

"It's all about the money" is a phrase we've all heard but I have never heard it more or thought about it more than I did in the last four years. I mentioned "heightened awareness" in the introduction, and along with the heightened awareness came heightened frustration. The truth is that it is all about the money, has been, and probably will be forever. Should it be though? Yes and no.

I completely understand the importance of money and the never-ending benefits, but money will bring out the best in people or the worst in people. The phrase "all about the money" can simply mean that it's what makes the world go around. Very true. It also can mean that it's the one and only thing people consider when making decisions in their lives regardless of the consequences to others.

Money and power are natural companions and certainly not bad when used for good purposes. There are many rich and powerful people in this country who do great things for many Americans and people in other countries. I have no problem with capitalism or anyone who makes an honest living making millions or billions. What I do have a problem with, however, is when it never seems to be enough. Many times money and power breeds entitlement and the combination of the three usually results in selfishness, greed, corruption, and crime.

Don't you think money was the main reason behind the Catholic Church cover up? It wasn't just about lawsuits but also the money they would lose from parishioners and contributors. So they were entitled to cover it up for decades?

The cost of running a political campaign is enormous, especially at the congressional level where there are no term limits. I mention term limits because obviously the longer a person is in Congress, the more money they need to raise. It is estimated that the average cost of a campaign for the U.S. Senate is about 10 million dollars and 1.4 million dollars for the House of Representatives. Some candidates in larger states can spend two or three times more. Contributions from large corporations and extravagant fund-raising events from lobbyists are common. Should we believe they do this out of the kindness of their hearts and not because they think they're entitled to something in return?

Almost every chapter of this book, those you've read and those to follow, gives examples of actions taken by individuals or groups based on entitlement. Almost always, money is the common denominator. One who had billions and whose case is the epitome of money, power, entitlement, corruption, and crime is Jeffrey Epstein. It is also an example of some serious deficiencies in our justice system, our democracy, our officials, and our citizens.

JEFFREY EPSTEIN

Jeffrey Epstein, Ghislaine Maxwell, Prince Andrew, Alan Dershowitz, Barry Krischer, Alexander Acosta, Ken Starr, Bill Clinton, Donald Trump...

This list of names represents just some of the people who were connected to Jeffrey Epstein in articles written about the sordid, disgusting, and highly illegal activities that probably took place for decades. **Not all the names on the list are people accused of wrongdoings.** Some have been accused, some connected because of their highly questionable actions in decisions to prosecute or not prosecute him, some were friends or at least acquaintances, and two are lawyers whose tireless efforts helped Epstein to escape justice over and over again. And one of those lawyers has also been accused of participating in alleged sex trafficking along with Epstein.

This case has had multiple TV documentaries

produced and at least one book written about it, with details of Epstein's life going back to the 1970s. There is a great deal of information, but as I'm devoting a chapter of the book (an important one), and not writing another book about it, I will do it in highlight form.

- There are questions about how Epstein made his money. It is reported that early in his career he worked for Bear Stearns and Towers Financial. While with those companies he was involved in insider trading and a Ponzi scheme, and allegedly stole 17 million dollars. He was never prosecuted. He eventually became a billionaire and there are still questions about how he acquired his fortune.

- In 1996, a victim of Epstein's goes to the NYPD and the FBI to file a report against him for sexual assault. Nothing was done. The victim eventually left New York and went into hiding. So two law enforcement agencies were notified and neither of them followed up?

- Fast forward to 2005, in Palm Beach, Florida. The mother of a 14-year-old girl calls

Palm Beach police to report that an older man was paying her daughter for some form of illicit sex. They take the allegation very seriously, find out that it was Jeffrey Epstein, and conduct a thorough two-year sex trafficking and sexual assault investigation.

- The police chief brings the information to the state attorney, Barry Krischer, who will be prosecuting the case. By 2007 they have uncovered about two dozen underage girls who were involved and issue a search warrant for Epstein's house. When they get there, Epstein is not there and his home is stripped of evidence including cameras and computers. Someone obviously tipped him off. The girls are now followed and threatened.

- Barry Krischer's eventual prosecution of this two-year investigation results in a misdemeanor with no mention of underage girls. Epstein posts bond and is free to leave.

- The Palm Beach police chief is understandably upset and decides to take the case to the federal level and goes to the FBI with the charges. The FBI investigation uncovers more victims which now total at least three dozen.

They even contact the woman who filed the charges back in 1996, ten years earlier.

- The federal prosecutor for the case is Alex Acosta. When the case goes to court, neither the victims nor their lawyer is notified and a secret non-prosecution deal is made with no federal charges: one count of prostitution, one count of soliciting a minor, and immunity for co-conspirators. Epstein spends about a year in jail, gets "work release," and is able to leave during the day to do whatever. When he gets out, his hard-working lawyers argue that he shouldn't be put on the sex offender list. Fortunately that judge couldn't be influenced or bought.

- Alex Acosta is later appointed Labor Secretary in 2017 by Donald Trump, a friend, or at least an acquaintance of Epstein.

- Much to their credit, the victims are not giving up and civil suits are filed. There is a Victims' Rights Act that says victims have to be informed of deals being made with the accused. In 2019, a judge rules that the victims' rights were violated and the government broke the law with the non-prosecution deal and light sentence.

- I'm not really sure how the government works sometimes, but if the government broke the law, and Alex Acosta was the prosecutor representing the government at the time, shouldn't he be somehow held accountable? Wait, it's not over.

- Epstein is arrested in July of 2019. Two days after the arrest Acosta resigns as labor secretary. Trump's quote regarding Acosta, "I'm with him."

- In 2020, the Circuit Court of Appeals rules that the victims' rights were not violated, sided with government, and overturned the 2019 ruling. So I guess Alex was just doing his job.

- It should be noted that Epstein had a private jet and numerous houses. Extensive camera systems were set up in all of them and reportedly in the bedrooms and the bathrooms. It's also no secret that he had numerous high-level friends and acquaintances. It's unfortunate that he was tipped off in Palm Beach because the cameras and other items he removed were very likely incriminating not only to him.

- Epstein is finally in jail at the Metropolitan Correctional Center in New York. He had been put on suicide watch for a while but then taken off and placed in the SHU (Special Handling Unit) where he was supposed to have a cellmate and be checked by guards every 30 minutes. They found Epstein hanging in his cell the morning of August 10th. On August 9th his cellmate had been transferred and was not replaced by anyone. The guards supposedly didn't check on him every 30 minutes because they were sleeping. Two cameras outside his cell malfunctioned. The medical examiner ruled his death a suicide.

- Some of Attorney General William Barr's comments on Epstein's death: "A perfect storm of screw-ups." "We will get to the bottom of what happened and there will be accountability." One year has passed and the only two people charged with anything have been the two guards. So I'm not really sure what he meant by accountability. The same accountability Barry Krischer received? The same accountability Alex Acosta received? The same accountability others accused along with Epstein received? The same accountability bank officials received for the 2008 crisis? The same accountability

Michael Flynn received? The same accountability Roger Stone received for lying to
Congress?

Note: Can we really expect greatness without accountability? The lack of accountability that is allowed in this country is disgraceful. This Epstein case
is like something you might expect to see in a third
world country. We're certainly not a third world
country financially, but how about morally? Have we
evolved morally or just found more innovative ways
and "legal" loopholes for immorality and injustice?

COMMENTS AND OBSERVATIONS

- Ghislaine Maxwell is now in custody and
  charged with perjury and conspiring with
  Jeffrey Epstein to sexually abuse minors.
  Victims say she was Epstein's "madame." In
  spite of all the charges and accusations going
  back to 1996, she was not arrested until July
  2020. That's already a travesty of justice.
  She knows everything about the abuse and
  everybody who participated with Epstein.
  She's scheduled to go on trial in July 2021.
  The government can't make up for previous
  screw-ups, but maybe they can get it right

this time. Let's not forget though that she supposedly has a lot of money so it shouldn't be difficult for her to find a "good" lawyer—that's if she even makes it to trial and doesn't hang herself.

- Prince Andrew has been accused of having sex with an underage girl and denies it. He's a known friend of Epstein and Ghislaine Maxwell and there is a photo taken of him, the then 17-year-old accuser, and Ghislaine Maxwell at Ghislaine's apartment. He denies the charges and says he doesn't remember the girl or the photo. Innocent until proven guilty.

- Alan Dershowitz was one of Epstein's lawyers and also has been accused of having sex with a minor and sued by his accuser. He has denied the charges and countersued. He represented O.J. Simpson and is one of Donald Trump's lawyers. Ken Starr is also one of Epstein's lawyers. They're sometimes referred to as "the dream team." They certainly are a dream team for wealthy accused felons. I'm really not sure what they are for the rest of us.

- Allow me to make a general statement about the law, prosecutors, and defense attorneys.

Innocent until proven guilty is the law. Everyone has a right to defend themselves and have legal counsel and everyone has the right to a fair trial. The truth and reality, however, is a little different. If you break the law, you're guilty. If you don't break the law, you're not guilty. That doesn't change regardless of what you can prove or not prove. So morally, if you're a prosecutor knowingly convicting an innocent person, or a defense attorney knowingly doing whatever is necessary to free a guilty person, you should be considered an accessory to that crime. I guess the laws aren't always based on morality or what's right and what's wrong.

- To be very clear, neither Bill Clinton nor Donald Trump have been accused of any crimes in connection with the Epstein case. They have been mentioned in the documentaries because they were both friendly with him. Bill Clinton flew on Epstein's private jet a number of times and was sometimes in the company of Ghislaine Maxwell and others. Epstein visited Mar-a-Lago a number of times and there are videos of Trump, Epstein, Ghislaine Maxwell and other women.

No crime there either. There is something there unsettling to me, though. If you're with him multiple times and spend time with him on his private jet, in his residence, at your club, and you were savvy enough and smart enough to become President of the United States, did you really not know what he was doing with underage girls? I guess you didn't because I'm sure you would have said something.

- *August 4th, 7:20 AM*: I came back to this chapter because I just saw an interview with Trump who was asked about Ghislaine Maxwell and said, "I wish her well." I won't put in writing what I wish for her. I wonder what he wishes for her alleged victims.

THE MAN IN THE
GLASS HOUSE

As you probably figured out by now, I'm not really a fan of the President (OK, that's an understatement). But I would like to share some thoughts with you on the months leading up to the election and the years that followed.

Donald Trump was a name I knew as a successful businessman who had a lot of money. I watched "The Apprentice" once. I didn't have any strong feelings about it only that his style did not appeal to me. As the years went on and he started to get more attention and became more vocal, he became even less appealing to me. When he declared that he would be running for president, I thought he was joking. He was so far from what I thought a president should represent that I couldn't comprehend that he was serious. And with his money and lifestyle, why would he want to be?

My next thought was that he just wanted to shake things up for a while and would eventually drop out. That didn't bother me, because I think things need to be shaken up with politics once in a while. Then the debates started and he was still in. Those debates really convinced me that he wanted no part of being president from the way he was acting: arrogant, rude, insulting, intimidating. He had no boundaries and went so far as to even insult the wife of one of his opponents. The comments he was making, as well as the Billy Bush video, showed me there was no doubt that he'll never win the primaries. Do you have any idea how humbling this is for me? I was wrong at every juncture, and I wasn't done yet!

So now he wins the primary election and becomes the Republican nominee. I was embarrassed for the Republican Party and annoyed with the people who thought this was the best choice of all the Republican candidates (I would eventually be embarrassed and annoyed with the Democrats, too, but didn't realize it yet). In a conversation with some close friends, I made the comment that I would vote for a monkey before I would vote for Trump. They laughed, but I meant it. I thought being stagnant for four years was better than going backwards.

And now to the election. The polls had Hillary

Clinton in the lead. I hadn't learned my lesson yet and thought the polls were way off. Trump would lose by a much larger margin than they were predicting. The polls were wrong and I was more wrong than the polls.

I went to bed on election night not too comfortable with what I was seeing but before it became apparent that he would even have a chance of winning. I had to, because if the unthinkable happened, I knew sleep would be impossible. When I woke up the next morning, I almost wished I hadn't. I was upset, and not just because Hillary lost, or I lost. I believed then, and believe now, that we all lost.

I remember begrudgingly watching the news that morning and hearing one of the national announcers say that since Trump won, maybe he will settle down and concentrate on being president and lead the country. Settle down and lead the country, are you kidding me? You're not changing the spots on that leopard. And now that he won, he's more embolden and will most likely get worse. Finally, my losing streak ended. It didn't make me feel any better though.

During the campaign and during his presidency, he often refers to opponents or people who disagree with him as liars. People who have testified against him are lying, "lying Hillary," "the lying press." Seriously, is that because of his own unwavering truthfulness? When he moved into the White House they should have changed the name to the Glass House.

We should probably take another look at presidential pardons, too. I'm not sure that being a longtime friend of the president and lying to Congress for him is sufficient reason for pardoning a convicted felon.

As there is some overlap in the chapters, this next topic could have been in some of the others but I decided to include it here.

Fiduciary: *Placing confidence or trust in someone else.*

In February of 2015, the previous administration, specifically the president, came out with the following statement. "Today I'm calling on the Department of Labor to update rules and requirements that retirement advisors put the best interests of their clients above their own financial interests. It's a very simple principle: You want to give financial advice; you've got to put your client's interest first." Financial advisors couldn't conceal any conflicts of interest and had to disclose all fees and commissions.

Now I don't know how all of you see this but you're telling me there wasn't already a law that prohibits them from doing whatever they want with our money for their own financial gains?

Moving on, it was approved in April of 2015 and the final ruling issued in April of 2016. Why a year later? Wait, it gets much better. Sorry, much worse.

New year, new administration coming. Early in 2017 in the first session of Congress, a bill is introduced to delay the implementation of the fiduciary rule for two years. The congressman who introduced the bill called it a "job destroying rule" and "harmful regulation." He wanted to give the Trump administration time to evaluate it.

So exactly who did he think this regulation was harmful to? I don't think it would have been harmful to me. I don't think it would have been harmful to the vast majority of Americans. If we had legislation similar to this prior to 2008 wouldn't it have helped to prevent the crash? I'm not a financial guy so maybe I just don't understand.

So the saga continued and even Alex Acosta got involved when he became labor secretary. He told the Wall Street Journal it would not be delayed beyond June 9th, 2017. The Department of Labor later filed paperwork to have it delayed further and the fiduciary rule was never implemented and vacated by the Court of Appeals in 2018. Acosta was still labor secretary at the time.

So why did I decide to put this saga in this chapter? I'll tell you how and when I found out about the fiduciary rule for the first time.

I'm retired, and in early 2017 went to meet with my financial advisor who is also a vice president of a fairly large bank. She apologized for some delays she was having with the computer system. She then commented that they had been changing some of their systems to comply with the new fiduciary rule but now that Trump was president, they knew it wouldn't be implemented. So if you're happy about it not being implemented, I wanted to be sure Donald got some of the credit for it.

And finally, I did eventually come to realize that I wasn't as wrong about Trump as I thought. Remember when I said I didn't think he wanted to be president? I don't think he did. I think he really wanted to be king. And be very careful America, the king has heirs.

10

"WE'RE ALL IN THIS TOGETHER"

No we're not!

Looking back, the day Donald Trump declared he was running for president, there was a line drawn in the sand, a deep one. It was a line that I believe divided this country more than I can remember in my lifetime. His followers sometime appear to be in a frenzy, and those who dislike him dislike him a lot. And that's putting it mildly.

But that's exactly how he likes it. That's his personality, that's his style, that's his plan, and that's why I didn't vote for him. Great is not a word I generally use to describe him but the best description I can come up with is "The Great Divider." And he's tireless about it. There's a lot of energy being wasted that he could be using to try bringing us together instead of constantly driving us further apart.

Are we all in this together when he makes racial comments? Are we all in this together when he makes sexist comments? Are we all in this together when he gives millionaires and billionaires tax breaks that will give them more millions and more billions?

Even in the midst of a world crisis, are we all in this together when he encourages us not to wear a mask, or when the vice president goes to the Mayo Clinic without a mask to visit coronavirus patients, or when Trump acts like he knows more about the virus than the medical professionals? It shouldn't come as a surprise to anyone that he keeps saying we have the virus under control. In his mind, as long as he doesn't have it, it's under control.

I'm not a medical professional, but after they find a vaccine for the coronavirus, I think they should look into a cure for the virus that has been destroying brain cells in this country for the last four years. I can point them right to the origin, too.

So for about five months now, I have been waking up to, and hearing throughout the day, from news anchors, politicians, sports announcers, athletes, entertainers, etc. "We're all in this together." It's inaccurate and annoying. Could you please consider finding another phrase? It's a request. I'm asking you not telling you. It's a free country.

THE IMBALANCE
AND CONTRADICTION
OF FREEDOM

As Americans, we take a great deal of pride in our freedom, and we should. The word "freedom" itself projects something very positive. Among those are the freedom of speech, freedom of the press, and the right to assemble. I'm not advocating taking away any freedoms but I do think there are some things to consider about the abuses of freedom. Maybe we should be considering some adjustments.

This is a delicate line, so I'm not referring to some slanted news that may come from major networks or radio broadcasts that favor conservative views or liberal views. The press can cross the line sometimes but they're a great watchdog. Can you imagine how far some people would go if they knew the press wasn't watching them? My concern is with the dangerous areas of extremism.

There are extremists who use free speech to their advantage in broadcasts and publications. Some of them promote hate and violence and others use it to knowingly spread blatant lies during political campaigns either about their candidates or their opponents. Millions of dollars are spent on ads spreading these lies and, even today, people seem to automatically believe them, or want to believe them.

We have a right to assemble peacefully and we should. I'll stress *peacefully* because when it isn't, you're working against the cause. There have been important marches and protests over the years for equal rights, the Women's March and The Me Too movement, gay rights, war protests, the environment, etc. all for legitimate worthwhile causes. The right to assemble also pertains to some groups whose very existence defies the laws of the land and the rights granted to Americans in the Constitution. And do we really expect a peaceful outcome when we allow protesters to carry weapons?

Americans have the right and the freedom (I guess) to not wear a mask during a pandemic even though it is recommended and encouraged by knowledgeable medical professionals.

Americans have the right and freedom to be

protected from other Americans during a pandemic and from getting sick or dying. Americans have the right to wear a mask without getting beaten up or having a gun pointed at them. Is this an imbalance and contradiction of freedom?

And lastly, we all have the right to be free from cruel and unusual punishment. I think four years of it is enough. I'm even concerned that if somehow he is elected to another four-year term, something disastrous could happen in this country or with another country, or both. Imagine what he'll try to do if he's not worrying about being re-elected? Actually he may even spend most of those four years trying to put an end to the two-term limit.

And for those subjects working for the king in the Glass House, I have two messages:

1) If you're under his spell, then hopefully you'll be gone along with him when he has to abdicate the throne.

2) If you get it, and have been trying to help minimize the insanity, the country owes you its gratitude. We're anxious to hear the stories, too, when you're no longer worried about being unemployed.

12

THE CANDIDATES

As I mentioned in Chapter Eight, I was upset the morning after the election. Not just upset, angry as hell. Too angry to make any rational judgments as to why Trump was elected. I'm embarrassed that I let it bother me as much as it did, but I needed to try to make some sense of it. How was he able to get over 60 million votes? And there were millions of very good intelligent people who voted for him. Right or wrong, let me share some observations.

For the bottom line of the election, one party gave us a candidate totally unfit to be president. The other party gave us a candidate who couldn't beat him. Trump and the Trump campaign outsmarted Clinton and the Clinton campaign. And whether he got the majority of the votes or not, he got the ones he needed to win.

We know about the millionaires and billionaires who voted for him but there certainly aren't 60 million of them. There were extremists who voted for him but fortunately not 60 million of them either. So where did the majority of the votes come from?

There were many voters on both sides who were voting against a candidate and not for a candidate. In hindsight, I was one of them. I wasn't thrilled about Hillary Clinton but more focused on what I thought were Trump's deficiencies. What I failed to recognize initially was that many people voting for Trump were focusing on Clinton's deficiencies. That's very troubling. So to both parties, shame on you, that was the best you could do? And don't go blaming the electorate for choosing them in the primaries. Your parties, campaigns, and candidates couldn't convince the American public that they had better choices? As disappointing as it is that we had to do this, this grouping is the one that got many of you off of my shit list, once I figured it out. That includes some of my friends.

Trump got a lot of anti-establishment votes simply because he was not a politician. But I see an anti-establishment vote coming from Americans who agree on some of the deep-rooted problems in this country. Americans who have issues with our democracy, our justice system, inequality, abuse, the widening gap between the rich, middle class and poor, the continued stalemates in Congress, etc. Looking at that list, did you really expect that he would correct any of these problems? I don't necessarily have a problem with the strategy of a non-politician, just the choice. It was like putting John Dillinger in charge of security at the U.S. Mint.

So what's left? The only other thing I can come up with is another group who honestly felt that the country would be better off with Trump as President. And I really wonder if and why they still feel that way. I have some questions for you to ask yourself. Do you feel that the vast majority of Americans are better off now than they were four years ago? Do you think there is less social unrest than there was four years ago? Do you think we gained more respect from other countries around the world than we had four years ago?

13

FINAL THOUGHTS

How many times have we stood with our hands over our hearts to recite the Pledge of Allegiance? We know the words by heart but do we take them to heart? Do we really think about the words especially in the second half of that one sentence: "...one nation, under God, indivisible, with liberty and justice for all?" Do we really understand what we're saying and do we mean it?

If after reading this book your only thought is "love it or leave it," you might consider that you're way more likely part of the problem than the solution. I know I'm somewhat of an idealist, but I'm also very much a realist. Nothing is perfect and won't be, at least not in my lifetime. That doesn't mean it can't be better though, much better.

As important as it is for me to put my thoughts on paper, I want it to be clear that in spite of pointing out issues, individuals, or groups that are a concern, I firmly believe that the vast majority of Americans are great people. The list includes all citizens, races, colors, poor, middle class, rich, law enforcement officials, D.A.s, attorneys, politicians, Republicans, Democrats, and independents. But within all those groups there are people who threaten our democracy, our justice system, and the values we should all be striving for.

As a realist I'm appealing to the majority. I don't think far right or far left is the way to go because we have to get back to working together. Our politicians have to get back to working together, too. There are basic philosophy differences in the parties as there have always been and our government is built on a system of checks and balances. Congress however is becoming more and more entrenched in partisan voting instead of reasonable compromise. It's almost as if their individual sense of reasoning shuts down and there are only two brains voting, the Republican brain, and the Democratic brain.

Nancy Pelosi and Mitch McConnell… thank you for your service. Don't you think it's time for the gold watch? Trust me, retirement is great. Unless you're pissed off about something.

Campaign rhetoric has become increasingly hateful and I'm convinced that it's one of the main contributors to that "line in the sand" that I mentioned before. This is not based on speculation; it's based on many years of experience and many presidential elections. There have been thirteen presidential elections since I have been old enough to vote. Sometimes my candidate won, sometimes they didn't. So life went on and I wait for the next election. Not in 2016 though, that loss cut deep.

> *If I'm the only one who felt that way then please forget everything I said in the book and just have me committed. If not, please continue because I'm not done yet.*

We live in a country full of opportunities. We should take advantage of those opportunities but not abuse them, and we should make every effort to see that those opportunities apply to all citizens.

There really is strength in numbers and we should not lose sight of one very important factor in our democracy—our politicians, and all government officials work for us. We pay their salaries, all of them. That's why they're called "public servants." I think they and we forget about that sometimes.

So I won't say "Let's Make America Great Again." It might be more accurate to just say "Let's Make

America Great." I don't think we're moving in the right direction, so let's start by getting back to where we were four years ago and work our way up from there. As Americans we need to regain some respect for ourselves and the respect of other countries.

Getting back to campaign rhetoric, I have a suggestion that I think should be a requirement for all political candidates regardless of the office. You can't make any promises or claims about anything you're going to do unless you tell us exactly how you're going to do it. Full disclosure.

A hypothetical example might be something like the candidate tells you he's going to build you a house with a fence or a wall or something and have your neighbor pay for it. But now he has to tell you *exactly how* he plans to build you a house with a fence or a wall or something and have your neighbor pay for it (I know that's too silly for anyone to believe, but like I said, it's hypothetical). There are two big advantages here. First of all, it would encourage and promote honesty from the candidates. Secondly, it would sure as hell shorten their speeches.

Although I have obviously criticized Donald Trump quite often in the book, he has only been President for four years. He was not the creator of injustice, inequality, inequity, congressional stalemates, or any of the problems that we're dealing with in this country. My criticism is that I don't think it was his priority to fix any of it and he actually made it worse.

For the election in November, if Trump wins, we know what to expect. If Biden wins, I guess we'll have to wait and see. Either way, someone needs to start making improvements in this country, and it should obviously start at the top.

Regardless of who wins, we, as citizens, should start to hold our elected officials more accountable. And if they don't make things better, we find replacements. Let your governor and representatives know what you're thinking and what's important to you. It's as easy as sending an email. If I can do it (and I do) you can do it too.

Get out and vote. Your vote in November may well be the most important choice you will ever have to make at the polls (or through the mail). In addition to all the other problems, there will still be the truly catastrophic consequences of the coronavirus, including our health and economic recovery. We need someone intelligent enough, and compassionate enough, to balance both. We have two choices. I hope we make the right one.

I told you all in the introduction that I would let you know if writing this book would help me to understand more or just make me more frustrated.

Researching details I wasn't aware of for some of the chapters certainly didn't make me feel any better. I am more frustrated, but probably just because I get more frustrated daily and not because I wrote the book. At this point I don't even know if the book will be published but I don't mind the time I spent on it because I couldn't go out anyway (I was concerned for your health and mine).

Before I let you go, and for the sake of total honesty, there was something in Chapter One that I need to clarify. I told you that at home there was no open verbal aggression or hateful comments towards anyone. I realized later that wasn't entirely true. We were avid Red Sox fans in our household. I think I recall some uncomplimentary comments made occasionally about the Yankees.

Thanks for letting me vent.

EPILOGUE

In the fall of 2016, my first book was published and released. The title of the book is "All Women Are Bitches: A Handbook for Men." The title is a little shocking, and was meant to be, but the contents are not what you would expect from the title.

It is officially classified as "adult humor, fiction" but many of the chapters in the book are actually true stories about events in my life. Even some that are outrageous enough that you would think they're fictitious. Much of it is really like an autobiography.

As I mentioned, the title was chosen for the shock value and also because I was very confident that the women who knew me knew that I respected them. I was also aware that some people wouldn't get passed the title and would never read it.

Prior to publishing, the focus of my concern when doing a market test was to see if women thought it was offensive. Women of different age groups read it, some knew me and some didn't. No one said they were offended by the title after reading the contents. No one mentioned in the book was mentioned without their permission. It was proofread, edited, and published by women. I'm telling you this for transparency because I want you to know about it.

In hindsight, I wish I had titled the book "Are All Women Bitches?" and made it a question rather than a statement. I wouldn't have changed the contents, but it would have softened the title slightly.

This book, "Liberty and Justice for All?" was written with facts that were checked and double-checked for accuracy that I hopefully got right. That was important to me. It also expressed my very honest feelings and opinions about a variety of issues—some you might agree with and others you may not agree with. I'm OK with that. No one is right about everything.

And finally, when I wrote the first book, I had absolutely no intention of ever writing another one. Writing it was enjoyable but I was done. When people asked me if I was going to write another book, I said no. But that was before Trump became the Republican nominee. After that, my answer changed to "Only if Trump becomes President." And my original title for that book (this book) was much more shocking than the title of my first one. I softened this one a lot. The contents didn't change.

ABOUT THE AUTHOR

Will Hanson is a Rhode Island native retired from manufacturing management. He enjoys spending time with family and friends and is a sports enthusiast. This is his second book that took about four months to write, after decades of experiences, and four years of awakening.